WHO'S HIDING... in Princess World?

igloobooks

Who's hiding in princess world?

Welcome to Princess Rose and Princess Lily's wonderful kingdom. There's lots of things happening all over the land, from big parties to fantastic sports competitions. Each picture in this book has all sorts of wonderful and interesting things for you to find. In fact, there are over 1000 things to be found in princess world! Princesses Rose and Lily are in each picture, so you'll need to find them first. Then, each page has little pictures to show you what else you need to look for, from strawberry pies to bales of hay and everything in between!

Princess Rose

Princess Lily

Can you find all of these items in the castle on the opposite page?

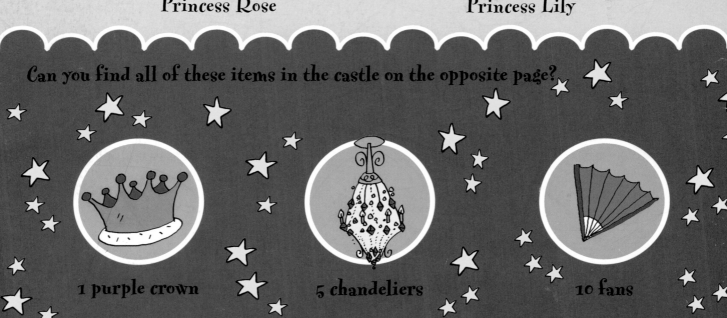

1 purple crown

5 chandeliers

10 fans

Palace Gardens

It's a busy day in the palace gardens.
Can you find Princesses Rose and Lily
amongst all of their friends.

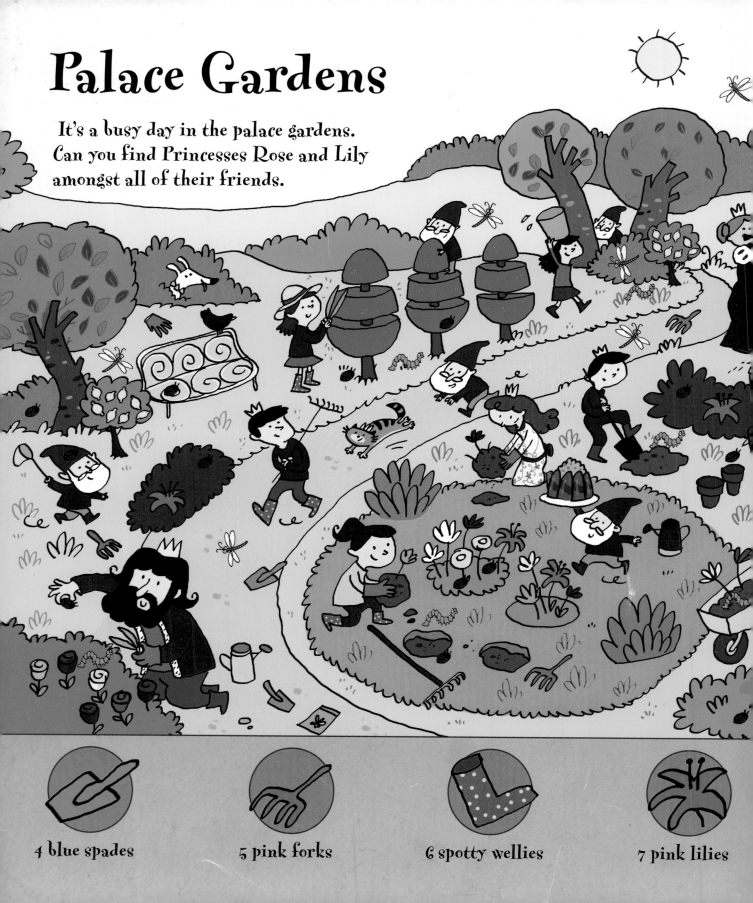

4 blue spades   5 pink forks   6 spotty wellies   7 pink lilies

Can you find all of these other items in the garden, too?

1 rainbow rose bush

2 purple hedges

3 lemon trees

8 green gloves

9 garden gnomes

10 orange caterpillars

20 ladybugs

Princess Picnic

There's a royal picnic at the palace today. Can you find Princesses Rose and Lily amongst all of their friends?

When you've found Rose and Lily, see if you can spot these things, too.

1 pink parasol

2 white rabbits

3 ice creams

4 purple birds

5 bananas

6 bumblebees

7 blue crowns

8 glasses of pop

9 yellow butterflies

10 pink cupcakes

20 pink leaves

Art Class

There's lots of things to make and do in the princesses' art class. Can you find Princesses Rose and Lily amongst all of the other artists?

4 paint palettes

5 pink paint pots

6 pairs of scissors

7 patchwork star

See if you can spot all of these other things in Rose and Lily's art class as well.

1 bowl of fruit

2 blue stools

3 sewing machines

yellow cotton reels

9 red balls of wool

10 purple hand prints

20 green paint brushes

Baking Fun

Rose and Lily are having lots of fun in the royal kitchen. Can you find them amongst all of the different chefs?

Now that you've found Rose and Lily, can you find these things in the kitchen, too?

1 pair of scales

2 egg timers

3 bags of flour

4 purple aprons

5 hand whisks

6 oven gloves

7 chef hats

8 apple pies

9 pink pans

10 wooden spoons

20 gingerbread people

Sports Day

Princess Rose and Princess Lily are hosting a sports day competition. Can you find them amongst all of their athletic friends?

4 red socks

5 megaphones

6 gold medals

7 blue javelins

Now you've found Rose and Lily, see if you can spot these things, too.

1 icecream stand

2 silver trophies

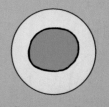

3 shot put balls

8 purple trainers

9 pink pairs of shorts

10 yellow t shirts

20 red flags

Dance Class

Rose and Lily have invited all of their friends to a royal dance class. Can you find them amongst all of the other dancers?

Now, see if you can find all
of these other items in the
dance studio, too?

1 disco ball

2 mice
in tutus

3 pink tutus

4 wall mirrors

5 blue chairs

6 red ribbons

7 kit bags

8 red apples

9 water bottles

10 pairs of
purple tights

20 white daisies

Horse Riding

Princess Rose and Princess Lily have taken their friends to see the horses. They are having lots of fun feeding and riding them. Can you spot the two princesses?

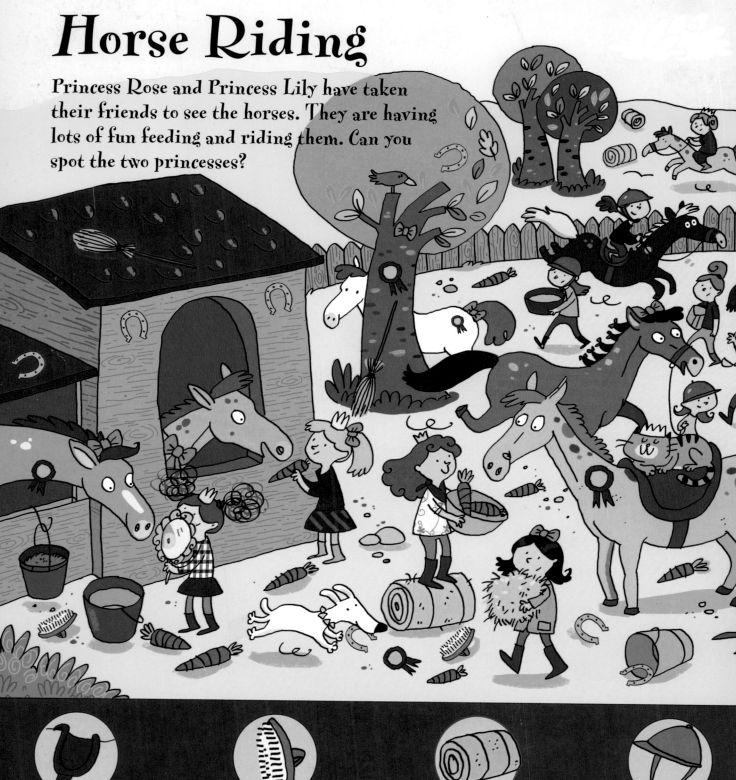

4 saddles on horses   5 pink grooming brushes   6 bales of hay   7 riding hats

Now you've found
Rose and Lily,
see if you can spot
these things, too.

1 white horse

2 green coats

3 brooms

8 brown boots

9 horse shoes

10 blue bows

20 carrots

Slumber Party

Rose and Lily are having a slumber party, all of their friends have brought sleeping bags and teddy bears. Can you spot Rose and Lily?

Now you've found Rose and Lily, can you find all of these other things in their bedroom?

1 hidden passageway

2 blue sleeping bags

3 rag dolls

4 hairbrushes

5 toothbrushes

6 teddy bears

7 purple pillows

8 cups of hot chocolate

9 stars

10 pink slippers

20 hearts

Shopping

Rose and Lilly have gone shopping.
Can you find them in the royal
shopping mall?

4 red lipsticks

5 pink combs

6 silver tiaras

7 blue purses

There's lots happening in the shopping mall, can you find these other items, too?

1 box with a purple bow

2 green shirts

3 hairdryers

8 purple bottles

9 white clothing tags

10 empty coat hangers

20 gold coins

Palace Ball

There's a royal ball at the palace this evening. Can you find Princesses Rose and Lily amongst all of their friends?

When you've found Rose and Lily, see if you can spot these things, too.

1 glass slipper

2 ice sculptures

3 dancing spiders

4 trumpets

5 strawberry pies

6 red balloons

7 pink bows

8 blue streamers

9 white candles

10 orange tiaras

20 rubies

Well done, you've found everything in Princess World! Now go back and see if you can find each of these extra items in every picture, too.

The King

The Queen

Palace ghost

Royal dog

Cat with crown

Bouquet of flowers

Pink jelly

Princess in a pointy hat

Gold statue

Royal shield

Hand mirror

How closely were you looking? Do you know which picture each of these items were in?

10 slices of chocolate cake

10 pink cardigan

10 red rosettes

10 stemmed glasses

10 purple hats

10 slices of pizza

10 tubes of paint

10 blue dragonflies

10 red shopping bags

10 rolling pins